Income Statement Basics
From Confusion to Comfort in Under 30 Pages

By Axel Tracy

ISBN-13: 978-1500142360

ISBN-10: 1500142360

Text Copyright © 2014 Bidi Capital Pty Ltd
All rights reserved.

Disclaimer
The material in this publication (the "book") and the information accessed through it is of a general nature only and does not contain investment recommendations or professional advice. The information is not to be relied upon as being accurate, complete or up to date. Axel Tracy (the "author") and Bidi Capital Pty Ltd (the "publisher") recommends that, before acting or not acting upon information contained or referred to in this book, readers should seek independent professional advice that takes into account their financial situation, investment objectives, particular needs and/or other personal circumstances. The information contained in this book is not to be used for any purpose other than income statement analysis and it is not to be construed as an indication or prediction of future results from any investment. Axel Tracy and Bidi Capital Pty Ltd do not offer financial, business or study advice. To the maximum extent permitted by law, the author and publisher disclaim all responsibility and liability to any person, arising from directly or indirectly from any person taking or not taking action based upon the information in this publication.

For Cepta, Declan, Ramona, Paul & All the Wonderful Family:
Thanks for showing me my history & the new family I had yet to meet.
For Phelim & the Ex-Telco Crew:
Thanks for giving me a chance to support and live a great life in Dublin

Table of Contents

About the Author 6
About accofina.com 6
Introduction 8
Example Income Statement 10
Housekeeping 13
   Income Statement Formatting 13
   Income Statement naming conventions 13
   Brackets within financial statements and other accounting documents 14
Quick Guide to the Income Statement 16
   Explaining the Income Statement in a Few Paragraphs 16
   Accrual Accounting: A Vital Concept in Income Statement Analysis 17
   The Income Statement linking into Other Financial Statements 18
Line by Line Analysis of the Income Statement 20
   Income 20
   Expenses 22
   Operating Expenses 27
   Income from Operations 29
   Non-operating income and expenses 30
   Income Before Taxes 30
   Provision for Income Taxes 31
   Equity-method investment activity 33
   Net income (loss) 35
   Earnings per Share Data 37
   Quick Summary & Lead into Comprehensive Income Statement 40
   Other Comprehensive Income (OCI) 41
Conclusion 49
Reference List 50

Extras **51**
  Book Excerpt 51
  Free Resources 55
  More Books by accofina 56
Author contact details and Review Request **58**

About the Author

Axel Tracy is an accounting and business student at the University of Technology, Sydney (UTS). He has a passion for his studies and has been accepted into the invitation-only Golden Key International Honours Society in recognition of having a GPA that placed him in the top bracket of students at his university. He is also an invited member of the UTS Honours Society.

He was employed by the University of Technology, Sydney to run PASS sessions. This was in the subject of Accounting Standards and Regulations; an undergraduate accounting subject that trains students to become familiar with Australia's implementation of International Financial Reporting Standards and the current Australian accounting standard regime.

Since April 2011, he has been the Founder & Director of Bidi Capital Pty Ltd, a holding company with two Internet businesses revolving around accounting & finance (accofina.com & RatioAnalysis.net).

Axel lives in inner city Sydney, Australia.

About accofina.com

accofina.com was launched in September 2013, and is a hub for accounting & finance knowledge and technology.

On the website you will find Kindle eBooks, iOS Apple Apps, MS Excel Spreadsheets & free Online Calculators all customized to assist putting academic accounting & finance knowledge, through technology, in the hands of businesspeople and investors.

accofina.com is part of Bidi Capital Pty Ltd, which is a company founded, directed and owned by this book's author, Axel Tracy.

Introduction

Whether you are running a business or analyzing and investment, you will no doubt be provided with the financial statements of the business. These statements can be daunting if you are unsure about how to read them, yet it is imperative to have some accounting knowledge if you want to know the true state of any business. The financial statements, in short, give you a condensed glance into the financial success of a business.

While country-specific regulation dictates which financial statements must be prepared by an entity, the three key financial statements are:

1) The Income Statement (The Profit & Loss Statement)
2) The Balance Sheet (The Statement of Financial Position)
3) The Cash Flow Statement

This eBook will cover the basics of (1) The Income Statement, and will be part of an eBook series of all three of these statements.

This eBook is not aimed at accountants or financial advisors, it is aimed at those who are provided with financial statements, yet do not have an accounting background. Warren Buffett has said that accounting is the "language of business" so this eBook should hopefully teach you a few key 'phrases' that will allow you to converse about, and navigate around, the income statement. Will you become an expert from this book alone? No, but the beauty of the key financial statements is that even a basic level of knowledge will allow you to make leaps and bounds when it comes to extracting value from the statements; in this case, the income statement.

Hopefully you should be able to tear through this read in one or two sittings, and you'll be prepped to make better business and investment decisions the next time someone hands you an income statement.

All the basics will be covered in under 30 pages, so this is more of a bird's eye view than an in-depth, in-the-trenches account of the income statement. The way the book is structured is also pretty simple. Firstly, we give you a real-world example of an Income Statement, and then we talk about some housekeeping issues and key concepts behind the statement. Then the real-bones of the book begins: we talk about each individual line item of the income statement, some accounting behind the scenes and finally some inferences you can draw from the account figures.

I am educated in accounting…and not educated in writing! I write because I like to help people learn accounting concepts…and I am passionate about accounting! I mention this because while I'd love to be a best-selling author, I know I will never become a best-writing author. The best I can hope for is that I become a better writer through each book being published over time. You can help me achieve these two goals:

If you want to help me become a better writer, please email me at axel@accofina.com and give me your suggestions for improvement. If you want to help me become a best-selling author, please leave a positive review for this eBook (and maybe a comment on how I helped you) on Amazon.com or GoodReads.com.

Time to get cracking!

Have a look at the Income Statement on the next page, don't worry if it looks all too foreign at this stage, just try and grasp some of the components and key groupings; we'll cover the detail later. Just know that you can keep referring back to this example Income Statement as we progress and hopefully by the end of the eBook you will feel very familiar with what is going on.

Example Income Statement

Amazon, Inc. (NASDAQ:AMZN)

**Consolidated Statement of Operations:
For 12-months Ending 31st December, 2012**

Extracted from Amazon's 2012 Annual Report (page 38) that was found within the Investor Relations section of Amazon.com.

(In Millions of USD)

Income:
    Net product sales $51,733
    Net service sales $9,360
        Total net sales   *$61,093*

Operating Expenses:
    Cost of Sales $45,971
    Fulfillment $6,419
    Marketing $2,408
    Technology & content $4,564
    General and administrative $896
    Other operating expense (income) $159
        Total Operating Expenses   *$60,417*

Income from Operations   *$676*

Interest Income $40
Interest Expense $92
Other Income (Expense), net   ($80)

Total Non-Operating Income (Expense)   *($132)*

Income before Income Taxes   *$544*

Provision for Income Taxes   ($428)

Equity-method investment activity, net of tax	($155)
Net Income (Loss)	*($39)*
Basic earnings per share	($0.09)
Diluted earnings per share	($0.09)

Weighted average number of shares outstanding:
Basic 453
Diluted 453

Consolidated Statement of Comprehensive Income:
For 12-months Ending 31st December, 2012

Extracted from Amazon's 2012 Annual Report (page 39) that was found within the Investor Relations section of Amazon.com.

(In Millions of USD)

Net Income (Loss)	*($39)*
Other Comprehensive Income (Loss):	
Foreign Currency Translation Adjustments, net of tax	$76
Net change in unrealized gains on available-for-sale securities:	
Unrealized gains (losses), net of tax	$8
Reclassification adjustment for losses (gains) included in net income, net of tax effect	($7)
Net unrealized gains (losses) on available-for-sale securities	$1
Total Other Comprehensive Income	*$77*
Comprehensive Income	*$38*

Housekeeping

Income Statement Formatting

The first housekeeping issue that is mentioned relates to the format of the Income Statement. The Amazon.com example statement just shown was drawn directly from their Annual Report, however you will find that different sources present the same information (the Income Statement) in different formats. So whether you are reading from annual reports, from Google Finance, from your broker or other information service, etc., you may find that each Income Statement is structured a little differently. Firstly, don't stress about this! You will soon have all the knowledge you need to navigate any format presented. I, for one, am used to reading Australian Income Statements, so Amazon.com being a US company and having US formatting forced me to take a 2nd look at it's formatting. But I, like you, didn't stress…the important idea is that whatever the format, in effect the same information is being presented. There is still revenue at the top, followed by expenses and finally a bottom line being net income (profit). Just think of it being like the differences between American and British versions of the English language: sure there are some notable differences, but these wouldn't stop you communicating in either country.

Income Statement naming conventions

While formatting issues based on individual systems is kind of easy to explain away, the naming conventions of the Income Statement is a little more confusing. For whatever reasons, the name given to the Income Statement has changed many times and rather rapidly too. You may find an Income Statement called 'a profit or loss statement', 'a profit and loss statement', 'a statement of financial performance', 'a statement of comprehensive income'…and even after researching this book and looking at Amazon.com's annual report: 'a consolidated statement of operations'. Just remember, whatever you name you come across, they are generally all the same thing. The national and international regulators just change the formal name (quite regularly), for reasons unbeknown to this author and many accounting professionals. The two most common names are 'income statement' & 'profit and loss statement' and if you are ever confused, just ask someone (or Google) if *that name* refers to an income statement or profit & loss statement. Apart from 'the statement of comprehensive income' (which we will address later), all names refer to exactly the (I mean identical) same document, it's simply a naming convention.

From here on in, and from the name of this book itself, we will be referring to it as the 'Income Statement'.

Brackets within financial statements and other accounting documents

Okay, this one may be obvious to you already, but since this is a 'fundamentals' book it should be covered. If you look at the example Income Statement you will see some figures surrounded by brackets, e.g. ($39). In financial statements and accounting terminology, bracketed figures simply mean a negative value, i.e. minus $39. This means the corresponding figures are also subtracted in any further calculations, e.g. $100 + ($39) = $61. There is one qualification I must mention: if you look at the "Operating Expenses" section of Amazon's income statement, you will see there are no brackets in this sections figures. However, an expense's 'natural state' is a negative value (i.e. you always subtract expenses from income), thus when it explicitly states that a figure is an expense it may not have brackets surrounding it. The key idea is that if a figure in the income statement could be *either* a positive OR negative value (e.g. Net Income), then brackets mean it is the latter: a negative value.

Quick Guide to the Income Statement

Explaining the Income Statement in a Few Paragraphs

Okay, so here comes the super-quick guide to the income statement that will act as a primer to the more in-depth analysis throughout the rest of the book.

The income statement is a performance report.

The income statement measures the performance of a business over a set time period based on its ability to earn profits over that set period.

While a balance sheet (another key financial statement) shows a snapshot picture in time, e.g. 21-Nov-2014, the income statement more closely resembles a 'video' as it measures performance over a set time period, e.g. 1-Jan-14 *through* 31-Dec-14. Note: the period need not be a year, it may be a month, quarter, half-year, etc.

How does it measure performance over set period?

Firstly it aggregates all sales and service revenue over the set period to create a 'revenue' figure.

Then it lists all the major expenses throughout the same period and groups them into easily understood accounts, e.g. admin expenses, marketing expenses, etc.

We then subtract the total expenses figure from the total revenue figure and what is remaining is that period's 'net income' (if the figure is positive) or 'net loss' (if the figure is negative). Ideally a business wants to have net income.

The benefits of income statement analysis are driven from how each line item, these being 'accounts' or sub-totals, shown in the income statement is used for further enquiry or action. For instance, you can analyse the ratio of net income to revenue to work out the profit margin, or you can analyse expenses over a number of income statements and see how expenses are growing or shrinking and make assumptions about management's cost control.

You may have just noticed how I mentioned that line items might be sub-totals (and not expense or income accounts). This is important to grasp as these sub-totals are also used for analysis. The idea is that the income statement is simply not just three lines: (1) revenue (2) expenses (3) net income. Instead the income statement has a number of sub-totals throughout (although they can change depending on the format of the document). Common sub-totals include (and we will go through all these in detail later on): gross profit, operating income & income before tax. Even below the net income figure we may have more sub-totals and line items depending on the size of the organisation, with earnings per share data being the most common.

Accrual Accounting: A Vital Concept in Income Statement Analysis

The concept introduced here is the concept of 'accrual accounting'. This means (in short) that all revenue and expenses are measured when they are earned (revenue) or incurred (expenses) and this is NOT necessarily when the matching cash flows occurs. In other words, within the income statement there are 'non-cash items': revenue and expenses on the statement when no cash has changed hands. I'll give a quick example to hopefully help with the explanation. Amazon.com pays its self-publishing authors 60-days after the end of the billing month, i.e. if you purchased this book in November, I as the author will be paid my royalty 60-days after the end of November (at the end of January). Now when should Amazon.com record this books royalty expense? In November when the royalty expense was incurred (i.e. you buying the book and Amazon incurring the author royalty expense) or in January (most likely in the next year's accounting period) when the author royalty was actually paid? The answer, under accrual accounting, is that the royalty expense for Amazon.com is recognised in the November, when the expense was incurred. The idea behind this type of accounting is that the income statement is a measure of economic performance and not just cash performance. It makes more economic sense to record the royalty expense in November when the book was purchased and the author's royalty was incurred. In this case, cash payment is an arbitrary date set by Amazon.com itself and not reflective of economic reality. Accounting reports should always try and reflect economic reality and not arbitrary choices of management or outside actors.

In conclusion, the income statement uses accrual accounting and reports all revenue and expenses over a set accounting/time period and measures the economic performance of an entity in relation to ability to earn net income (profits).

The Income Statement linking into Other Financial Statements

As mentioned in the introduction to this book there are 3 main financial statements: the Income Statement, the Balance Sheet and the Cash Flow Statement. One of the unique and advantageous qualities of these three statements is that they are all linked to one another and you can feed aspects of each into sections of others, both for calculation uses and for accuracy checking.

When it comes to the Income Statement, the Net Income figure links into the equity section of the balance sheet. Specifically, net income minus dividends equals this year's retained earnings increase. And last year's retained earnings (on last year's balance sheet) plus this year's retained earnings increase equals the new balance sheet figure for the retained earnings account.

The other link to the balance sheet is more conceptual rather than arithmetic. You will see in the next sections formal definitions of income and expenses from the International Accounting Standards Boards, or IASB. The IASB is an international rule-setter when it comes to financial accounting and reporting and when it comes to their definitions of income and expenses you will see that they are based on the definitions of assets, liabilities & equity and also on the rules of double-entry accounting. We will not delve into these issues now, but just remember that the formal definitions (of income and expenses) provided by the formal rule-setter (the IASB) are linked to the balance sheet concepts of assets, liabilities and equity.

If you are a little unsure of your skills when it comes to the balance sheet, please consider another of my Kindle books in this series, **Balance Sheet Basics: From Confusion to Comfort in Under 30 Pages.**

Line by Line Analysis of the Income Statement

Income

"Income is increases in economic benefits during the accounting period in the form of inflows or enhancements of assets or decreases of liabilities that result in increases in equity, other than those relating to contributions from equity participants"
- *IASB Conceptual Framework 4.25(a)*

Here is that IASB definition of income that was mentioned in that previous section. And while definitions of assets, liabilities & equity do not really fall in a book about the income statement, the key intake for a beginner from the above definition is "increases in economic benefits during the accounting period in the form of inflows". And breaking this down…and mind you, the IASB is famous for mind-bendingly convoluted prose…the definition of income is based on the idea of the accounting period (the length of the 'video' or set period) and the inflows or increase in economic benefits during this period, and 'economic benefits' can just normally be boiled down to 'money'.

As I'm writing this, I am beginning to question the benefit of including this definition in a "basics" book. The IASB or FASB (the US equivalent) are at the top of the pyramid when it comes to the study of financial accounting, so I believe that their definitions are the purest source of knowledge. But when it comes to fundamental-level learning, the definition may make the concept more complicated than what it really is. So here is the solution: if the above definition (a possibly my explanation) is something you can grasp, then brilliant! If your eyes are glazing over and you are now less certain of your skill level than you ever were, then don't fear! Why, because here is the 'basic' concept: *Income is money you earn from selling goods or selling services (keeping in mind the accrual accounting concept).*

Looks get past definitions and look at real-world examples:

Turning back to the Amazon.com 'Income section' of the example Income Statement you will see "Net Product Sales $51,733" and "Net Service Sales $9,360". Simply, since the Income Statement set period (accounting period) is the 12-months Ending 31st December, 2012, the line amounts shown, and just mentioned, mean that Amazon.com sold in the ordinary course of business $51,733m worth of products in the year, and note these are tangible ("touch-able) goods (products) like SLR Cameras, Bedding products, etc. And the 2nd line item, correctly referred to as an 'account' (so the 2nd income 'account' shown) simply means that Amazon.com sold $9,360m worth of services throughout 2012; services like subscriptions to Amazon Prime, streaming movies, etc. The difference being is that a 'service' is an experience, process or benefit that Amazon will offer or perform for you, while a 'product' is something Amazon will deliver to you. These are my definitions of product vs. service and I've modified them to apply to Amazon, so you may find different definitions for these depending on where you look. It's also important to note the goods and services lie on a spectrum. That is, at one extreme of the spectrum lie products that are tangible goods you receive in return for payment and the other extreme are services that are pure experiences offered by the seller's staff. In between, there can be different mixes of goods and services: think about an airline, they offer the service of transport but also offer products such as drinks and meals during that service. While this discussion may be somewhat off on a tangent, it does illustrate that the income statement often arbitrarily breaks down data into specific categories to allow comparability between all income statements.

Note: all the Amazon figures quoted above are "Net" figures, so it can be assumed that this is total sales less refunds, returns and other amounts reducing gross sales. And try to remember the 'accrual accounting' concept we talked about earlier.

A quick word on revenue: revenue is defined as income earned in the ordinary course of business. For example, a bookshop earns revenue selling books, but if that bookshop sold the company car for a profit, this may have earned "income" (the profit on the sale of the company car) but it wouldn't be classified as revenue as a company car sale is outside the ordinary course of business for a bookshop. In reality, 'income' (in the top section of the income statement) and 'revenue' are often used interchangeably and 'income' is often a shorthand way to say profit or net income, so it is important to look at the context as to how each of the phrases is used to understand which definition to apply.

So pulling this all together: The top section of the income statement (also known as the 'top line' by some journalists, analysts and others) lists the total sales revenue of the business in question over a set accounting period. The total sales revenue within the income section is often broken down into product and service distinctions and totals are given for all three: net product sales revenue, net service sales revenue and the aggregate total sales revenue or income. Underlying all this data is the concept of accrual accounting (described in the Quick Guide section), which means all the totals given refer to income *earned* in the period and *not* necessarily the cash received from sales.

Expenses

"Expenses are decreases in economic benefits during the accounting period in the form of outflows or depletions of

assets or incurrences of liabilities that result in decreases in equity, other than those relating to distributions to equity participants."
- *IASB Conceptual Framework 4.25(b)*

Above is the definition of expenses according to the IASB and again it has links to the balance sheet even though expenses are within the income statement. The quickest way to make sense of this obtuse definition is to look at the similarities between it and the IASB definition of income in the last section. You will see rather quickly that the two definitions are mirrors of each other and the language is almost identical (it's just mirrored language). From this you can conclude that expenses are the opposite of income and essentially represent the opposite effect within the Income Statement, that being they subtract economic benefits (money) during an accounting period.

If again these definitions are not your preferred method of learning, the simplest way to look at it is that expenses are the ongoing costs to run the business during a set accounting period. They are things like office rents and marketing expenses. The things you need to pay for in the ordinary course of business. Using a basic definition again and mirroring the earlier statement, we can say that the 'basic' concept is: *Expenses are the monies you spend or incur while in the ordinary course of selling goods or selling services (keeping in mind the accrual accounting concept).*

Expenses take up most of the remaining Income Statement aside from the calculation results. That is, they lie beneath the income section and roll all the way down to the net income figure (aside from calculation results along the way).

Looking at a real-world example you can see Amazon's expenses (within the included Income Statement) include operating expenses, non-operating expenses and tax expenses (tax provisions to be specific).

Before we go any further, it is time to talk about a number of different formatting options to describe how the expenses are set out in the income statement.

Alternative 1a 'Descriptive Format':

This alternative is just the option that Amazon.com has taken in our example. The descriptive format displays the revenue figure and simply subtracts all expenses to leave a net income figure.

You can see with Amazon.com that they have set out their Income Statement with an 'operating expenses' section that provides most of the detail of their day-to-day operations, which is directly below the revenue figures. Amazon divides their ordinary expenses into certain categories (such as Cost of Sales & Fulfillment) and simply allocates all ordinary expenses into one of these categories.

Note: It is often important to read the Notes to the Financial Statements (the 'fine print') to get further clarification into the brief (1-page) set of results are calculated and allocated. After doing this with Amazon, I found out that they even break down their depreciation expenses into their respective operating expense categories, such as some depreciation for 'Fulfillment' and some depreciation for 'Technology & content'. Many businesses separate out depreciation and amortization and it was only through reading the fine print (the 'Notes') that I learned that they used this particular accounting policy. Different accounting policies can have very wide implications for financial statement analysis, so the more comfortable you are with getting your head around the basics, the more you should delve into the financial statement Notes to get even more detail.

Okay, getting back to topic, in short: the descriptive format shows revenue minus expenses equals net income.

Alternative 1b 'Functional Format':

The next common format is the functional format income statement. While essentially displaying the same information (all income statements essentially show the same thing), the functional format inserts a 'gross profit' section just below the revenue section. That is, revenue minus 'cost of sales' equals gross profit, and only then the rest of the expenses are listed. The functional format separates out cost of sales and gross profit from all the other expenses. This format is common in retailing and manufacturing business (as 'cost of sales' play a large influence) while the descriptive format is more common in service businesses (as 'cost of sales' play a smaller role).

Here is a quick aside if you are unsure as to what 'cost of sales' are: Cost of sales, a.k.a. Cost of Goods Sold (COGS) or Cost of Revenue, are those expenses/costs which are incurred to get inventory that will later be resold. Perhaps in a retailing business cost of sales are the prices paid to wholesalers for the goods the retailer sells. Or perhaps in a manufacturing business, cost of sales are the costs/expenses incurred in manufacturing products that will later be resold.

Do you see why cost of sales and gross profit figures are vital indicators (and hence the functional format) for businesses that hold inventory? Costs of Sales are unavoidable (and often large) expenses for some businesses so their measurement and ongoing management are very important. And gross profit figures (Revenue minus Cost of Sales equals Gross Profit) are also very important as they represent the starting point to meet all other expenses and net income.

Below the gross profit section, the descriptive format and functional format are the same. It is only the inserted gross profit section that makes the income statement a functional format statement.

Alternative 2a 'Single-step' format:

The 'Single-step' format is not an add-on from descriptive and functional formats, but is a separate format type to be compared to 'Alternative 2b Multi-step'.

The 'Single-step' format is a description given to income statements that generally only offer one calculation (hence single-step). This one calculation is revenue minus expenses equals net income. Thus the only three sections that have aggregate totals are revenue and expenses and the single step is to calculate one minus the other.

These types of income statements are normally only used with smaller and more closely held businesses. The simpler style is adequate for the smaller business or businesses without too many outside observers.

Alternative 2b 'Multi-step' format:

It is easier to understand alternatives 2a and 2b when you compare them to each other, so hopefully after you read this section the previous alternative will make more sense too.

The Multi-step format is what is used in the Amazon example income statement. It is a multi-step format statement because there are a number of calculations running down the page (hence, multi step). Looking down the example statement now, you can see that revenue minus operating expense equals Income from Operations, then you subtract non-operating expenses to calculate Income before Tax and only after subtracting tax expenses can you calculate a final Net Income figure. Do you see how this is multi-step? Each calculation down the page feeds into the next calculation.

Multi-step format statements are common in larger companies and especially those that are public companies and/or listed companies. This is because there is much more analysis that can be gleamed from a multi-step statement. You can perform analysis and draw conclusions from any and all of the steps. This is beneficial when there are many outside parties who need to analyse the statements, for example when the company is listed on a stock exchange and there could be vast quantities of people interested in the details of the company income statement.

Alternative 3+ 'Management accounting' and other formats

While not as common as the other above alternatives, there are still a few other ways to format an income statement.

One you may come across is when expenses are broken down based on management accounting costing principles. For example, expenses can be broken down into fixed and variable costs. This example would be most useful for internal management when formatting isn't regulated at all. For reference, fixed costs are those that cannot be avoided in the short-term (hence they are fixed), variable costs are those that vary based on the level of production or activity (hence they vary and are called variable costs).

The key take-away from this alternative is that unless a format is dictated by a regulator or exchange, there is really no limit onto how you structure your own income statements. As long are there are revenue and expense sections and a final net income figure, you can design how to represent the statement. The important thing is that whatever format is chosen, it has to help the statement's reader make better business and investment decisions.

Operating Expenses

Now that we have dealt with a number of formatting options, let's return to the Amazon example we are working through. Understand one statement to begin with and branch out from there.

Directly below the revenue section you will find 'Operating Expenses'. Taking on board what was discussed earlier about expenses in general, operating expenses are those expenses that are incurred during the normal business operation. In Amazon's case, operating expenses would involve things like marketing the Amazon website with banner ads, or perhaps the cost of the servers that manage the Amazon website. You have to ask yourself: 'is this expense incurred during day-to-day Amazon management, that being the business of being an online retailer and technology service company?' When you can say 'yes' to this question then that expense will fall somewhere in the first expense section of 'Operating Expenses'.

Looking deeper, you can see the operating expenses are broken into categories. While I will not waste time by explaining the different between a 'Technology' expense and a 'Fulfillment' expense, the key take-away is the analysis that can be drawn from the category breakdown figures. You can see that Amazon's marketing expense are approximately half of the technology expenses; what can we draw from this? Perhaps Amazon's focuses on 'technological excellence' over 'marketing spin'? Or on the flip side, perhaps Amazon is giving up 'customer acquisition' and choosing 'technological fancies' instead?

In regards to which answer is which, I can't say, but what we can say now is that we have a starting point for filtering all Amazon Inc. company info we hear of from here. We also have benchmarks and proportions to measure against all future income statements, and see if there is a change in strategy (i.e. a deliberate cutting of costs, or growth in expenditure, in particular categories). We can also compare relative totals between Amazon and competitor companies, for example: perhaps we could infer that eBay Inc. has a bloated management structure if their 'General and Admin' costs were six times larger than Amazon's given similar revenue totals between the two (Note: I don't know the accuracy of this size-comparison statement, it's just an un-researched illustration).

It's this type of analysis where we get the most value from income and other financial statement analysis. Now, don't get me wrong, there are limitations to what we can draw from an income statement alone, let alone when we start dealing with accounting manipulation. But from generally a single page

document (or a few pages for all statements) you can't beat the succinct summarization that financial statements provide, and the guidance they offer for further inquiry. You have to keep asking yourself, "What is behind this figure?".
Remember, the income statement is a *summary* of the period, so ask yourself what the story may be behind each summarization.

Income from Operations

Now that we have the revenue data and the operating expenses data, we can calculate the Income from Operations. This is simply the former minus the latter. In the case of Amazon, it is $676m. Why is this result important? Simply: because this is the performance of the business at carrying out its core activities. Strip out the odds and ends, irregular occurrences and other financial complexities, the income from operations is simply how good Amazon was (in their case) at being an online retailer and technology provider for the previous twelve months. After all, isn't this something we want to know? You'd be a little concerned as an investor if Amazon constantly had accounting profits based on equity investment returns (for example) but could never get positive income from operations for being an online retailer. Sure you may not be too concerned as an investor if these accounting profits meant the stock kept on rising, but still, you would most likely have invested as an online retail play and based your decision on Amazon putting itself out there as a leading retailer...not the (hypothetical) equity investment vehicles that is leading to its accounting profits.

Long story short: income from operations is a one-line performance measure about how well a business succeeded in running its core operations. This one line is not the whole story, but it's valuable to be aware of, keep an eye on, and understand.

Non-operating income and expenses

Remembering what we were just talking about in the last section, the next section of the income statement should be self-explanatory, or at least easy to grasp with a little explanation. Taking on board the concepts of revenue/income and expenses, non-operating income and expenses is simply those income and expenses that do not form part of the day-to-day, normal operations of the business.

You can see from Amazon's income statement that these non-operating entries involve interest income and expense as well as a catchall "other" account. Amazon isn't a financial institution, they don't 'normally' get involved in the business of borrowing and lending money; this isn't their day-to-day operations. But that doesn't mean they have zero interest income or expenses and we must account for it somewhere. So it falls into the non-operating income and expenses section. As for the catch-all "other" account, we can just assume that there are a number of other individually immaterial transactions that fall outside day-to-day Amazon business and are too small, or too widely dispersed to even categorize, except to put them in an "other" account.

Pulling these three accounts together, they are summed and presented with another one-line item: Total non-operating income or expense; in Amazon's case this is a loss of $132m. Now this one-line is not really that significant in itself, but where it draws most of its value is that this total is subtracted from Income from Operations to result in a more significant value, the one-line item Income Before Taxes.

Income Before Taxes

This total derives it's greatest use when you are an outsider and you are comparing multiple businesses, for example if you are analyzing stock market investments and you have a choice of not only Amazon but also Wal Mart, eBay, Barnes and Noble and any other retailer, for example. While net income (after tax) is the "bottom line" of any business, you will find the tax liability and payments of any business will be slightly different to any other. I'm not just talking about the total tax figure, but more about tax rates, tax credits, tax rollovers from previous years, etc. For almost each and every business tax complexities will be different each year and different between businesses.

Why does this have an impact? Because tax policy and tax rules are set outside the organisation. The governments set the rules and this is well beyond the control of management; those we are trying to assess with our income statement analysis. Further, if you as a stock analyst are trying to compare multiple companies in multiple countries, the tax rules and consequences on the "bottom line" can be like night and day across borders.

So if we are trying to assess the performance of a company and its management, shouldn't we strip out the parts of the income statement where management and the company have no control (i.e. Tax issues)? And this is what the Income Before Tax total provides: a profit figure measuring the performance of the business before things get complicated by outside taxation issues. Strip these complications out and you can now compare performances for companies in different tax jurisdictions and/or different tax statuses with different tax implications.

Provision for Income Taxes

Move on to the next section of our income statement we will find the line item Provision for Income Taxes. In the simplest way to explain it, this is an expense that represents how much was allocated for income taxes this year.

It is a little more complicated than that quick explanation. For instance, this figure may not represent the final tax bill for that year. This is evidenced by the fact it is termed as a provision. In accounting terminology a "provision" is similar to a liability (e.g. a tax liability) but isn't an 'exact' liability. As the IASB (the accounting rule-setters we talked about earlier) defines, a provision is a liability of uncertain timing or amount. Thus from this definition we can see that the provision for income tax relates to an uncertain amount or uncertain timing of payment. These two conditions fundamentally contradict the rules for recognizing a true liability, hence the provision concept.

Further complications into that simple definition include the fact that the figure doesn't represent how it was allocated, e.g. by way of putting away funds or actually paying taxes. The provision is just an accrual entry (remember accrual accounting from the Quick Guide section?) to recognise a probable debt that will eventually be paid. The figure is no guarantee or amount or timing of payment. The expense here is simply recognition that tax expenses are incurred in the same period as income is earned and also the opposite entry of balance sheet recognition of taxes owed within a double entry accounting system. Want to know more about balance sheets and double entry accounting? Check out another book in this series: **Balance Sheet Basics: From Confusion to Comfort in Under 30 Pages.**

Lets not over complicate this line item, the simple definition will suffice and just further think about it as how much tax expense was incurred on the income the business earned in the year or accounting. And a tax expense is like any other expense we discussed earlier except that it's paid to the government and not suppliers or employees. Anything deeper than this can be for your further studies beyond a 'basics' book.

Equity-method investment activity

This next section of our income is heavily influenced by accounting rules and terminology, so hang in there, as this line item can be quite substantial for some companies.

As you know many businesses invest and take stakes in other businesses. The example you are probably most familiar with is a subsidiary, i.e. this company is a subsidiary of that company or that company has this many subsidiaries. We are going to start our explanation with the parent, subsidiary concept and then move onto our current line item focus. A subsidiary is defined as a business in which a parent has 'control' over that subsidiary. 'Control' is the key concept here. The parent can ultimately dictate the financial and operating policies of the subsidiary and this is normally achieved through owning a majority of shares or having a majority of board seats. Now when a company has subsidiaries there are set rules on how to account for the subsidiaries income, expenses, assets, liabilities and equity. These rules are called 'consolidation accounting' and in the end the financial statements of parent and all it's subsidiaries are blended together (in a quite complicated accounting procedure) to form one set of 'group' financial statements. In other words, from a quick glance of a group's income statement you can't see any specific line items for the subsidiaries. There is no line item or definition between parent and subsidiaries, they are blended to form a single set of statements.

Taking this on board now let's turn our attention to the line item equity-method investment activity. This is another way to account for investments in other businesses. But these investments, shown within our current line item, are not subsidiaries where the parent has control, instead we use this different accounting method when a company has 'significant influence' over another business. 'Significant influence' over the financial and operating policies of a company is the key criteria. And we don't call the influenced company a subsidiary, instead the accurate term is to refer to them as 'associates'. So in our example, the appearance of this line item proves that Amazon has an investment in at least one associate.

So what exactly is significant influence? How can we define this? Sadly, I can't give you a black and white definite answer. But a rough guide that normally holds true is when an investor company owns 20%-50% of the equity of the investee company. This normally allows significant influence over the 'financial and operating policies' of a company.

Still with me? Now let's get to that line item and its respective amount. When an investment in an associate is made, an asset on the balance sheet is created with the value of the cost of that investment. For (hypothetical) example, Amazon buys 30% of company ABC for $1 million, therefore on the Amazon balance sheet an asset (with a $1 million value) is recognised on the Amazon balance sheet. Over time company ABC makes profits, losses, pays dividends, etc. which all affect the equity of company ABC. While the exact accounting behind it is complicated and beyond the scope of this book, all these changes in company ABC's equity are proportionally transferred to the asset that Amazon recognised on its balance sheet. For example, if company ABC made $200,000 profit (an increase in equity) in 2015, then Amazon asset would increase by 30% times $200,000 or $60,000.

We are almost there: so, finally, what is represented on the income statement of Amazon (we've been talking lots about assets and balance sheets)? The figure on the income statement is simply Amazon's share of the profits of its associate(s). Simply collect the net income figures of Amazon's associates, multiply these by Amazon's ownership share, sum/aggregate all these and we at last have the figure of a $155m loss.

So, while the concept and accounting behind is a little harder to grasp, understanding this investments and the line item is important. Considering Amazon's income before tax was $544m, a $155 loss from its associates is a pretty hefty slap.

And depending on the strategy of any particular company, its investments in associates could be much greater with an even greater exposure to potential losses or gains.

Net income (loss)

Okay, here we are almost finished! We have reached the net income figure. This figure is the company's profit, its net income: the bottom line, as it often referred to as.

While the concept of profit as defined by the international accounting standards board is more complicated than it needs to be, the more digestible idea is that profit, or net income, is simply income (revenue and gains) minus expenses. And these details are exactly what we have been going through in this book. So in Amazon's case, we take the income before taxes figure and subtract the income tax expense and the equity-method accounting expense to achieve a net loss (the figure is in brackets) of $39m.

Net income is the simplest and purest measure of performance. It is a summary of all the businesses activities for the period wrapped up in a single figure. And when the "profit motive" is the fundamental goal of corporate entities in a capitalist system, you can see why net income becomes the "bottom line" when it comes to the performance of the business. Note, the term "bottom line" is synonymous with being a representation of what's "most important" for many aspects of life, it's easy to forget that the term is based on the accounting income statement and the net income figure normally resides on the actual bottom line on the page/statement.

So now that we have this figure, what can we do with it? Like many financial statement items, it's best value can be drawn from comparison with other items of financial statements, both current and past statements. Although it is important to note that no other figure on the income statement can quite stand alone as a source of informational value as the net income figure can, as there is much we can do with knowing this figure without reference to other data.

So let's get to the point, what can we do with this figure? We can assess the trend in performance by looking at previous net income figures; is this figure increasing steadily over time? Or do we have a 'growth' company and it's increasing rapidly? Ideally, unless management made a conscious decision to scale back in size, we wouldn't want this figure falling over time. I mention this often, but it's important to use key pieces of data as not ends in themselves, but the grounding for further inquiry. So using some sort of trend analysis as an example, we may next inquire into what has changed, or remained the same, over the period of analysis. For example, if the net income trend has stopped increasing and has now fallen, ask yourself why might this be so. Is there new strong competition? Have the general economic conditions changed? Has a new management strategy backfired? In short, listing every possible reason for a hypothetical change in net income trend is a little limitless and futile. Just remember that a valuable piece of data can become more valuable when compared against similar data in different periods and that individual figures are great to be used for further enquiry.

Other comparison relationships that can make the individual figure more valuable is when you compare the net income figure to similar businesses or competitors within the industry. You can see if any particular measure of performance is inline with everyone else, and thus not really that unique or special, or whether it stands out from the crowd and represents something unique about that particular business and is worth further investigation.

The next technique you can use has been mentioned earlier. You can compare the net figure to other line items within the financial statement, whether this is the income statement itself or the balance sheet or the cash flow statement. There are particular ratios, such as the profit margin (net income divided by sales revenue), that are common within financial statement analysis, but the honest truth is that there is no real limit on what ratios you can calculate and which you put emphasis on. If you can justify value from the ratio of net income to another piece of data, then there are no rules against doing this. While the common ratios have become mainstream because of their regarded value to analysis, it is unique information that may give you an edge over others: as no one else may have this particular insight. Just make sure that before you run off placing too much emphasis on any ratio (this could apply for any analysis technique) that you test the relationship with your desired outcome and perhaps give it time and multiple occurrences before you risk too much of your investments or business on it. As with many pursuits, you need to try things in the real world to become skilled, but make sure you can walk before you run.

So get out there, start walking and start applying some analysis techniques using the net income figure, but as for this book we are going to move onto the EPS and shares outstanding data which sits after the net income figure.

Earnings per Share Data

This section of the book actually focuses on the next four pieces of data (or line items) below the net income figure, as opposed to just a single piece of data. We are now looking at Basic earnings per share, Diluted earnings per share and the two lines incorporating 'weighted average number of shares outstanding' (both basic and diluted).

For many investors the absolute net income figure, which we just discussed, is not too easily distinguishable and valuable without some of the deeper analysis we talked about. Often as investors, when we need a more distinguishable, or more of a headline, figure, and for this we can look at earnings per share (EPS) data. This figure represents a quick and handy glance at what our shares (ownership) did for a particular period. We, as share owners after all, want to know what earnings we're generated on each share. The EPS data gives us this information. It is a quick and simple calculation that allows comparison against all possible stock market opportunities (that is, all stock market companies offer EPS data so we can easily compare all investment opportunities).

You will also find that EPS data is what most if the major media company's report in their stories. Whether it's Bloomberg or the Wall Street Journal or any other, you will find that they generally report company earnings via an EPS figure. This feature alone makes it imperative for any investor to become familiar with this piece of data.

Further, many professional stock market analysts (those that provide company forecasts and reports, buy or sell recommendations, etc.) base their earnings estimates using an EPS figure. For example, you often here something like this is the financial media: "the consensus earnings estimate for company XYZ this quarter is $1.27 a share". This is simply another way of saying that the forecast EPS is $1.27. Due to the significant stock price changes that can be caused by meeting, beating or missing analyst forecasts, it becomes even more important to understand EPS figures.

The final aspect I will mention before moving onto our Amazon example is that there is a relationship between EPS data and stock prices. While it is different in every single, individual company case, it can be generally said that the higher the EPS figure, the higher the stock price. Due to the fact that stock investors are indirectly purchasing a claim to the earnings of a business when they purchase shares, it is no accident that shares with higher earnings attached to it (i.e. higher EPS) fetch higher prices in the stock market. If I quote exact data today it may become stale in a book without exact date references, but I will say, if you want proof of this general rule, go to Google Finance online and pick a stock with a price less than $10 and find its EPS data, then go look up Berkshire Hathaway Inc. 'A' Shares and see what it's stock price is and its respective EPS data. What you will find is no accident and will be, in general, repeated throughout the stock market in varying degrees.

Okay, let's move onto how EPS data & 'weighted average number of ordinary shares outstanding' are calculated and then how this applies to our Amazon example.

Simply, EPS is calculated by dividing net income by the (convolutedly named) weighted average number of ordinary shares outstanding. Basic earnings per share is Net Income divided by Basic weighted average number of shares outstanding and Diluted earnings per share is Net Income divided by Diluted weighted average number of shares outstanding. Not to difficult, huh?

Weighted average number of shares outstanding isn't too difficult to grasp either. It is simply a calculation of the average number of shares outstanding over the year (or period). Because new shares may be issued, or shares bought back or cancelled, the number of shares outstanding often fluctuates up and down over a year. To take account for these fluctuations, the figure and term, weighted average number of shares outstanding was created to give an average number of shares outstanding. It is 'weighted' because each level of shares outstanding may last for different lengths throughout the year. The weights represent the portion of the year for each level of shares. For example, there may be 1000 shares outstanding in January and then on the 1st of February 200 new shares are issued and the number of shares outstanding remains at 1200 over the rest of the year. In this example we can make a calculation to determine the Weighted average number of shares outstanding: 31 days at 1000 (all of January) and 334 days at 1200 shares outstanding (the rest of the year). Thus the calculation to apply weights is 31/365 times 1000 plus 334/365 times 1200. The result is 1183 and therefore in this example the weighted average number of shares outstanding is 1183.

Now to the terms 'basic' and 'diluted': Basic refers to the number of current, standard level of shares. The diluted level refers to the number of shares outstanding if all stock options

39

or convertible bonds were exercised. For example if there were 1000 basic shares outstanding but the CEO of the company had stock options that entitled her to 300 shares (if exercised) then the diluted level of shares outstanding would be 1,300.

So now we have covered all the fundamentals, we can look at the Amazon example. The first thing you'll notice is that basic and diluted weighted average number of ordinary shares outstanding is the same. While this makes it easier for us to understand our example, this situation is often not the case. Anyway, knowing this we can look at our example income statement and see the Net Loss of $39m divided by 453m weighted average number of ordinary shares outstanding results in the basic and diluted EPS of $0.09.

Quick Summary & Lead into Comprehensive Income Statement

Well, we have now finished with our core analysis of the income statement, well done! You could finish your reading here and be adequately prepared to work your way around a small business income statement or still perform a lot of analysis of the income statement of a listed company. We've basically covered the tried and tested fundamentals of income statements. I hope you get out there and start looking through more and more income statements and apply what you have learned and start developing your own systems of analysis.

There is still one more section to this book, though. In recent times, the financial accounting standard setters have added another section to the income statement. This new section is a little complicated conceptually, but thankfully if you do struggle here... or I struggle to explain it well, I can assure you that what we have covered so far in this book will keep you in good stead for the large majority of occasions when you need to understand the income statement. This new section is the

Statement of Comprehensive Income which is included after our example main Amazon Income Statement. The Statement of Comprehensive Income comprises changes in 'Other Comprehensive Income' or OCI. So, if you are ready and want to complete the final step of this introductory journey, let's get to it!

Other Comprehensive Income (OCI)

Other comprehensive income and this measure of performance now needs to be reported for large or important companies either in a separate statement in itself or as part of a Statement of Comprehensive Income. In the Amazon example, they have chosen to include a 'Consolidated Statement of Comprehensive Income' directly after their income statement. This statement reports the changes in other comprehensive income (OCI).

What

So what is OCI? It is actually a little difficult to summarize in a nice, neat fashion. It can encompass a number of different items, but essentially all items in OCI "reflect re-measurements as a result of movements in a price or valuation". What does this mean? In general, apart from a few exceptions, assets or liabilities of the company can and often do get revalued as part of the accounting process. The financial accounting standard setters decided that these revaluations may not be *real* gains or losses to be shown in the main income statement, but should instead be recorded as gains or losses in a catch-all section which is OCI.

Here's where it gets even trickier: some "re-measurements as a result of movements in a price or valuation" DO, in fact, go into the main income statement, some do not (and instead go into OCI) and some go into OCI and are then 'recycled' or transferred into the main income statement at a later date....confused? Yeah, me too. And we are not alone: even the financial accounting standard setters, the mighty rule writers at the top of the pyramid, cannot give a definite answer about which revaluations ("remeasurements") appear where. Some situations as easier to understand than others (I'll give a quick example in the 'Why' section next) but if at this introductory level you need something to hold onto, then the best answers is to read the titles of the individual line items, remember that they are the double-entry accounting treatment of "movements in price or valuation" in assets or liabilities and then try to play devil's advocate of why they are not included in the main income statement. Remember they are all accounting treatments, and those within the organisation ultimately decide all accounting policy and treatments, so the rule setters have limited the accounting policy choice of some internal managers (or internal accountants) to avoid perverse incentives.

Why

I just said OCI has been used to avoid perverse incentives of internal managers. This is only partly true and definitely not the full truth. The truth is that accountants are supposed to be conservative. No, that's not only a funny stereotype, they are supposed to "anticipate no profit and provide for all possible losses". Accountants are supposed to be the cold shower for the CEO's hopeful optimism. Okay, take this board as step one.

Step two, let's again look at the formal definition of income we defined early in this book, *"Income is increases in economic benefits during the accounting period in the form of inflows or enhancements of assets or decreases of liabilities that result in increases in equity, other than those relating to contributions from equity participants."* That is, income represents increases in equity from increases in assets or decreases in liabilities.

Final step: ultimately we must account for *anything* that fits that definition of income. And in complex entities with complex accounting there are a number of activities that do, in fact, fit this definition but breach the conservatism principle or do not otherwise truly represent management's use of company resources. For example, if company ABC on the NYSE held stock in a speculative, micro-cap company that doubled in value in one day, would that be *real* income for ABC? Did management have any control over the quick spike in this asset's value? ABC's assets and equity did both go up over that one day! Some conservative accountants might argue this is NOT real income until ABC actually *sold* the stock at the new value and *realised* the income.

This previous example of income (or losses) is just one of many that can fit the formal definitions of income or expenses but fail the conservatism test of being *real* or fail to truly represent management decisions. And yes, there can be losses in OCI, they are just the same circumstances as OCI income but reversed. And because there are so many possibilities of these *unreal* income and expenses, OCI was created. OCI is hoped to show ALL transactions that fit the definition of income and expense, but aren't allowed to be shown in the main income statement.

Ideally, the inclusion of OCI is supposed to give a more complete picture over the performance of the entity, even if outside management control. The OCI data is included if it is relevant to helping make better decisions based on the Income Statement.

Here's another quick example to show why some income isn't allowed to be shown in the main income statement. This is the example in 'Why' I referred to earlier and also one that is aimed at avoiding perverse incentives:

Earlier we talked about company ABC owning a speculative stock, but as speculative or small cap as it might be, if it's a listed stock then there is a public price that is hard to argue with. Let's now imagine company XYZ that owns 5 office buildings. Under a particular accounting rule, company XYZ may revalue these office buildings on the balance sheet up to 'fair value' when fair value is higher than the current 'book value' (the value the office buildings as currently stated on the balance sheet). Now this isn't a formal definition of this particular accounting rule, but we can still continue with the argument: what is 'fair value' of these 5 office buildings? There is no public exchange to get accurate prices, there could be multiple values dependent on which appraiser values the buildings, and some buildings may have steel foundations while all other comparable buildings may have concrete foundations. You see what I'm getting at here? The ultimate determinant of what fair value to put on these buildings is up to company XYZ's accountant…part of internal management! What if company XYZ was about to miss analyst earnings forecasts of $1m? Wouldn't it be easy for company XYZ's accountant to revalue the office buildings up by $2m? Assets go up $2m (the increase in fair value of the buildings), equity goes up $2m as the double-entry balancing adjustment, and voila (!) net income goes up $2m (remember the formal income definition) and company XYZ beats the analyst earnings forecasts! This is a rather simple demonstration but you'd be surprised how often it occurred until the financial accounting standard setters dictated that this type of income under the revaluation model (that particular accounting rule) must be recognised in OCI instead of net income. Specifically, assets would still go up $2m but the double entry balancing adjustment *must* go in an OCI equity account (called revaluation surplus) instead.

Detail

Okay, in this 'Detail' section I am only going to give a brief overview. I will try and make the overview comprehensive in scope, but the analysis will not be deep. A deep, detailed tutorial would in effect become an advanced financial accounting course. I will give you a list of most possible items in OCI and the go through the Amazon example that only touches on a few of the possibilities. My best advice: if this 'Detail' section confuses you and you want to know more or if this section's analysis is not deep enough, then please let this be an invitation to further your accounting knowledge journey. The Internet, other more advanced books and educational institutions all offer deeper, more advanced and often better education than this book. So let me be brief in this section and, if desired, continue your knowledge journey with new sources.

When I first learned about other comprehensive income (OCI) it involved taking a couple of particular accounting courses within a degree and studying the Accounting Standards Handbook which is a 1600+ page book detailing the rules of the IASB (no, we didn't have to read the book cover to cover in our courses). What I did learn though was that there is no specific list, no index item or section that was solely focused on OCI. Instead, rules for using OCI were spread sporadically throughout the whole Handbook. So when I approach writing this section in this book I cannot reference an exact list of all items that fall within OCI. What I have found though is a couple of good websites (**www.ifrsbox.com** & **www.accountingtools.com**) that both do indeed try and give a direct list. So here is a blended list of their offerings. According to these websites, which I tend to agree with, this is an itemized list of all accounts that could appear in the OCI section:

1) Available-for-sale securities fair value changes that were previously written down as impaired
2) Available-for-sale securities unrealized gains and losses
3) Debt security unrealized gains and losses arising from a transfer from the available-for-sale category to the held-to-maturity category
4) Foreign currency gains and losses on intra-entity currency transactions where settlement is not planned or anticipated in the foreseeable future
5) Foreign currency transaction gains and losses that are hedges of an investment in a foreign entity
6) Gains and losses arising from translating the

financial statements of a foreign operation
7) Changes in revaluation surplus related to property, plant and equipment
8) Actuarial gains and losses
9) The effective portion of gains and losses on hedging instruments in a cash flow hedge
10) For financial liabilities designated as at fair value through profit or loss: fair value changes attributable to changes in the liability's credit risk

Note: This is not my own list. It is a blend of two lists from the websites listed above. I have provided these sources (also included in the Reference List at the end of the book) for you for your own review. These websites offer a 'good option' when trying to offer you, the reader, a comprehensive list when I list like this is not offered in the Handbook.

With that qualification note covered, and the list given, you will see why I am not going into each item in detail. A detailed discussion is simply beyond the scope of an introductory level and would break the short, concise format I want this book to hold. I encourage you to research, study or simply Google each item on your own: best wishes.

Now for the Amazon example, where I will briefly cover some of the detail: Let's look at our Amazon Consolidated Statement of Comprehensive Income. All of those listed items in the Amazon example really only cover Item (2) and Item (6) from our just mentioned 'exhaustive' list. Let's go the statement one by one.

Firstly, Amazon begins with the Net Income figure of a $39m Loss taken from the main profit or loss statement that we covered, it then moves onto the OCI section.

First up, it talks about Item (6) "Gains and losses arising from translating the financial statements of a foreign operation" or as Amazon puts it "Foreign Currency Translation Adjustments, net of tax". This amount (of $76m) occurs because balance sheet items (assets, liabilities and equity) of foreign operationsare translated at different foreign exchange rates than income statement items. Some parts of the income statement (such as tax provisions, depreciation and OCI) are reliant on balance sheet items, while we are trying to present income statement items in this section. If you translate foreign currencies at different rates and at different times, the equality link between the balance sheet and the income statement are broken. No longer does last period's equity plus income (minus losses) equal this period's equity. When breaking this equality breaks accounting rules then a new temporary, 'trick' balancing account is added: Foreign Currency Translation Adjustments. This is ultimately a 'nothing' accounting other than a dummy account to make sure all accounting rules hold after foreign currency conversions (translations) have taken place. It is just a balancing account in the balance sheet and it can change the value of balance sheets items and thus sometimes creates formally defined income or expenses. Therefore since it does create formally defined income or expenses, it must be shown somewhere in comprehensive income.

The next section Amazon has is "Net change in unrealized gains on available-for-sale securities". This section (thankfully) is a little more self-explanatory, in fact we sort of covered it in our company ABC example just a short while earlier.

First, we have the account: Unrealized gains (losses), net of tax, of $8m. This is simply unrealized (unsold) gains or losses of securities that are held by Amazon that are available for sale (or, could be sold at any moment without restriction). So a stock listed on the NASDAQ possibly held by Amazon would be available for sale as there is a ready market for these investments and nothing restricting any possible sale, while a security in an unlisted company (perhaps share capital in startup) may not be available for sale as there is no liquid market for this of security, in effect it's sales is restricted.

Next up in the "Net change in unrealized gains on available-for-sale securities" section we have: Reclassification adjustment for losses (gains) included in net income. This account is a reversal of the previously discussed account for security gains or losses which *have* been realised, i.e. the securities have been sold, the income becomes 'real', is taken out of OCI and then transferred to the main income statement. So, hypothetically, if the following year all those unrealized gain securities (remember it was $8m) were sold the following for $10m, then the following year's "reclassification adjustment" would be a gain of $8m (which would be in brackets: see the line item and formatting description in the example statement) and the actual $10m gain would be in the main income statement, as described by this particular line item.

From here all the remaining items in the Statement of Comprehensive Income are totals and summations, and thus are pretty easy to grasp.

Firstly, we have a total of the "Net change in unrealized gains on available-for-sale securities" which is simply the sum of the previous two totals which we ran through. Next up we have a Total of Other Comprehensive Income, which is just a sum of Foreign Currency Translation Adjustments and Net change in unrealized gains on available-for-sale securities. This is the total (given by the name) of the 'mini' income statement that is the Statement of Comprehensive Income. And finally we have a total that is the bottom line of the main income statement plus the total of other comprehensive income. This Comprehensive Income figure is the final line item on our full, comprehensive income statement.

Conclusion

Well, that's it! We've covered the general income statement and briefly gone over the statement of comprehensive income. You are now armed with the core knowledge to begin income statement analysis, congratulations!

Thank you for your purchase of this book and thanks even more for the time you have given to reading it. I do hope you feel confident with what we have gone through and you are now more prepared when you come across your next income statement. I have enjoyed writing this concise book, but the true value is the belief that I have helped you on your accounting knowledge journey, or even helped you start it. I will say that like a lot of other subjects, with financial statement analysis you learn the most when not only studying but also when applying what you have learned. There are an enormous amount of free sources of income statements out there, especially on the internet, so make sure that you belief in yourself and have a crack at performing some income statement analysis. No one has perfect knowledge: not you now, not me ever, nor my accounting professors, but this should not stop any of us from applying, testing, refining and repeating what we know about financial statement analysis. This book has hopefully given you the belief that you are now ready to start your own analysis and system development.

Thanks again, best wishes and I'll leave you with a quote from one of my idols, Warren Buffett: "Time is the friend of the wonderful business, the enemy of the mediocre." It's now time to use the income statement as part of your determination into which side of this quote your target business falls within.

Best of success!

Axel

Reference List

Pozzi, C & Shying, M 2011, *Accounting Handbook*, 2011, CPA Australia & Pearson Australia, Melbourne.

Horngren, Harrison, Bamber, Best, Fraser & Willett 2007, *Accounting*, 5th edn, Pearson Australia, Sydney.

Business Insider 2014, *18 Brilliant Quotes From The Greatest Investor Of All Time*, Sydney, viewed 19 May 2014, <http://www.businessinsider.com.au/warren-buffett-quotes-2012-8?op=1 - time-is-good-only-for-some-13>.

Luecke, R.W., Meeting, D. T., 1998, 'The FASB introduces new rules for comprehensive income.', *Journal of Accountancy*, May 1998, <http://www.journalofaccountancy.com/Issues/1998/May/luecke.htm>

PWC Blog 2009, *What exactly is 'other comprehensive income'*, viewed 14 May 2014, <http://pwc.blogs.com/ifrs/2009/09/what-exactly-is-other-comprehensive-income.html>.

Accounting Tools 2014, *Other Comprehensive Income*, viewed 14 May 2014, <http://www.accountingtools.com/other-comprehensive-income>

IFRS Box 2014, *2 Steps to Distinguish Other Comprehensive Income from Profit or Loss and Changes in Equity*, Bratislava, viewed 14 May 2014, <http://www.ifrsbox.com/how-to-distinguish-other-comprehensive-income-from-profit-or-loss-and-changes-in-equity/>

Extras

Book Excerpt

Income Statement Basics is part of series, Financial Statement Basics, and the first book of this series was Balance Sheet Basics. You will often find within the book you just read that we have referred to the balance sheet. Thus, if you are just beginning you quest for knowledge within financial statements, then I recommend you consider Balance Sheet Basics that is also written by Axel Tracy (author of Income Statement Basics).

While an income statement deals with income, expenses and profit or loss, the balance sheet deals with assets, liabilities and equity.

Below is one section from Balance Sheet Basics.

Taken from:

Balance Sheet Basics: From Confusion to Comfort in Under 30 Pages
By Axel Tracy

Available to Buy Now from Amazon.com

Assets

"An asset is a resource controlled by the entity as a result of past events, and from which future economic benefits are expected to flow to the entity"

- IASB Conceptual Framework: Chapter 4 The Framework; paragraph 4.4(a)

The definition above is the 'complicated' definition of an asset, which I mentioned earlier. The definition comes from the International Accounting Standards Board (IASB), a financial accounting standards (rules) organization that sets the standards for all nations who follow international accounting standards.

Breaking the jargon down, the definition is not too complicated. An asset is something that is "controlled" by a business (like a factory) due to a "past" transaction (buying the factory), which causes a flow to the business of "future economic benefits", i.e. income will be derived from using the asset in the future (the factory will produce goods in the future that will be sold for income).

Technically, anything that fits inside the above definition could be called an asset. And these are what sit at the top of the balance sheet.

The key idea is that an asset is acquired and/or held by a business in order to generate, or access, cash from it in the future.

Generally, the convention is that assets are listed in order of liquidity down the balance sheet. That means that the most liquid assets (e.g. cash) sit at the top of the list of assets and the least liquid (perhaps an oil transport tanker) sit at the bottom. The term "liquidity" simply refers to the ability to turn the asset into cash. If the asset is considered highly liquid, then it is easy to convert to cash, if it considered highly illiquid, then it is hard to convert to cash.

Taking on board these key ideas, have a look at the Amazon Inc. balance sheet. What can you deduce from the assets listed in this financial statement? Are the highest asset values located near the top, implying lots of liquid assets? What does each asset value tell you about the Amazon business model, e.g. does it use high levels of equipment fixed assets, or have high levels of accounts receivable?

I cannot stress enough the concept of asking yourself, when you look at the balance sheet, "what does this tell me?" If you spend enough time analyzing the accounts, you can start to draw inferences about the business. For example, I just mentioned testing whether the accounts receivable is high, you could spend time comparing the accounts receivable balance over time (over multiple balance sheets) and test if this asset figure is rising or falling. A fall may mean that the business is improving its collections operations, or maybe that it is tightening its credit policy. When you draw one conclusion, you can often check its validity by looking at other sections of the financial statements.

While this last paragraph is more about financial statement analysis rather than understanding balance sheets, I hope you can appreciate the idea that while this concise eBook can help you get your head around a balance sheet you can always learn more and get more value from all financial statements.

Current Assets

Now that we've covered the definitions of 'current' and 'assets' we can take a little more time looking at specific current assets.

Remembering that the current assets are the most liquid since they are at the top of the balance sheet, you will soon realize that many current assets are, in fact, monetary in nature. That is, they are defined and measured in terms of currency. Where the Property, Plant & Equipment (a non-current asset) value represents something like a factory in a city, many of the current assets specifically represent a currency value (like 'Cash' or 'Accounts Receivable').

Let's add a quick finance concept before moving onto analyzing current assets...

We mentioned that asset liquidity refers to assets ability to be converted to cash. You may ask why a business would give up liquid assets (which can pay the invoices that come in) for less liquid assets (which may involve a lengthy process before using them to pay the invoices)? The answer lies in the generally accepted principle that a business (or even an individual) gives up liquidity in order to (hopefully) obtain a higher return from the asset. Look at Amazon Inc's top two current assets, 'Cash & Equivalents' and 'Short-Term Investments': now both are highly liquid (they both sit right at the top), but from their order you can see that cash is more liquid than short-term investments. Now that makes sense, you can simply go to your bank and make a withdrawal from Cash today, yet you may need a few days or few weeks to sell the Short-Term Investments and wait for the delayed settlement to realize their cash value. But look what also makes sense: do you expect a higher return from your checking account interest rate (Cash & Equivalents) or from your corporate bonds (Short-Term Investments)? While not specifically fitting into the 'Current Assets' section alone, this lesson is important to remember for the rest of this eBook and your own balance sheet analysis.

Now with this lesson under our belt, what can we learn from the current assets section of a balance sheet? One, of many, things we can draw is that we can test how 'secure' the business will be at maintaining its operations. As mentioned, you can generally only pay the business' bills with cash, and you only really ever go out of business if you can't pay your bills. So knowing this we can look at the structure of a business' current assets. If 'Inventory' is too high, it may mean that the entity can't sell is stock or maintain optimal stock levels in-store. If 'Accounts Receivable' is too high then it may mean that the entity can't collect its debts adequately. Yet, if the more liquid current assets are too high, then this may mean that the entity is forsaking a higher return on its assets for the sake of having lots of cash and short-term investments. Knowing what to look for, and how to interpret values, will take practice, but even within these past few pages you can begin to start telling the story of the business from what may have been an almost 'foreign' set of line items and values.

Free Resources

www.ifrs.org The International Accounting Standards Board and International Financial Reporting Standards Foundation have a joint website. Often these Standards and rule-setting board are referred to in my books, so why not go directly to the source yourself. Here you will find a wealth of information regarding financial accounting. It may seem a little complex or overbearing early on, but once you become more familiar with accounting jargon, then this source is the top of the pyramid.

www.fasb.org The Financial Accounting Standards Board is the US equivalent of the IASB. The FASB are the rule-setters in an American context and create the generally accepted accounting principles, or more commonly referred to as GAAP.

www.coursera.org/course/accounting A world-leading MOOC provider. It has a free introductory financial accounting course from the University of Pennsylvania. This course requires no prerequisite accounting knowledge and covers far more than most books.

www.google.com/finance A great hub of company information, including financial statements. It has global sites and some great financial tools such as a portfolio tracker and stock screener as advanced as anywhere in the public world.

www.investopedia.com A great financial education website, from financial markets to personal finance. While a lot of it revolves around investing, one if its core products, the dictionary (the "pedia") is an invaluable reference for novices to professionals alike.More from accofina and Other Books

More Books by accofina

These accofina Books are Available from Amazon

Balance Sheet Basics: From Confusion to Comfort in Under 30 Pages

Ratio Analysis Fundamentals: How 17 Financial Ratios Can Allow You to Analyse Any Business on the Planet

331 Great Quotes for Entrepreneurs: You Dream, You Believe, You Create & You Succeed

Axel Tracy's (Founder of accofina) Amazon Author Page

www.amazon.com/-/e/B00ED77BJ4

Free PDF micro-eBook

If you visit **accofina.com** and look on the Homepage or within the Book Menu, you will find the ability to download a Free Micro (15-page) PDF eBook, again authored by Axel Tracy.

"Accounting: Foundation Inputs & Outputs" is a 15-page micro-book, while brief, will give you a grounding into the Inputs and Outputs of a Financial Accounting System. Specifically, the book covers the three main financial statements (outputs) and the theories behind entering data into your bookkeeping system (inputs).

Free MS Excel Spreadsheet

Again if you visit **accofina.com** and look on the Homepage or (this time) within the Spreadsheet Menu, you will find the ability to download a Free MS Excel Spreadsheet.

The Spreadsheet performs Time Value of Money calculations and provides the formulas behind each calculation. The Time Value of Money theory explains how the value of a certain sum of money, say $1,000, depends on when you receive this sum. E.g. $1,000 received today is valued higher than receiving $1,000 in 2-years time; because if you receive the sum today you can invest in a risk-free asset and in 2-years you will receive the initial $1,000 plus the interest (return) from the risk-free investment.

Author contact details and Review Request

You can contact me anytime and for any reason at any of these contact points. Tell me if you enjoyed the book, or if you could suggest anything for a 2nd edition.

Email: **axel@accofina.com**

Facebook: **facebook.com/accofinaDotCom**

Twitter: **@accofina**

Google+: **https://plus.google.com/+Accofina**

Amazon Review Request:

As mentioned in the introduction, I'd love to get an Amazon Review from you if you enjoyed, and got value, from this eBook.

Positive Amazon Reviews are worth their weight gold and could possibly propel my little business beyond my wildest expectations.

If you did get a positive experience from this eBook, I'd deeply appreciate it if you could spare a couple of minutes to Rate the eBook (on this eBook's Amazon product page) and maybe leave a positive Comment. Thanks again.

GoodReads Review Request:

After getting a few GoodReads reviews and signing up for this social network myself, I'm starting to see that this site could also be a great location for book reviews and referrals for possible sales.

Again, if you had a positive experience from this book, got value from your monetary investment and would like to share this with your GoodReads Friends, please feel free to post a Review on my Author Page:

www.goodreads.com/author/show/7450542.Axel_Tracy

Positive feedback is crucial for any author and the network effect of GoodReads *could* help your mates out, and *will definitely* help my business out. Cheers.

www.ingramcontent.com/pod-product-compliance
Lightning Source LLC
Chambersburg PA
CBHW021039180526
45163CB00005B/2191